ARCHITECTURE
IN AMERICA

A PHOTOGRAPHIC HISTORY FROM
THE COLONIAL PERIOD TO THE PRESENT

BY WAYNE ANDREWS

REVISED EDITION

NEW YORK ATHENEUM PUBLISHERS 1977

FOR ALAN AND FRANCES BURNHAM

Library of Congress Cataloging in Publication Data

Andrews, Wayne.
    Architecture in America.

    Bibliography: p.
    Includes index.
    1. Architecture—United States—Pictorial works.
I. Title.
NA705.A53 1977   720'.973   77-4273
ISBN 0-689-70549-2

Published simultaneously in Canada by McClelland and Stewart, Ltd.
Manufactured by Halliday Lithograph Corporation, West Hanover, Massachusetts
Designed by Harry Ford
First Revised Edition

PREFACE

Der Traum ist alles, doch nicht alles Traum. GERHART HAUPTMANN

The worst books of all, as André Gide did not hesitate to remind us, are those written with the best of intentions. My own intentions in publishing this new and revised edition of *Architecture in America* are honorable, so honorable that a word of apology may be in order. My ambition is to present a photographic survey of American architecture that will be fair to the point of view of almost every generation. I know that I shall fail, for like many people I remain a perpetual adolescent and shall never stop nursing my misgivings about what passed for taste in the 1920s when I was growing up. So there will be no illustrations of Art Deco skyscrapers nor of the work of Ralph Adams Cram, then so highly regarded for his prudent churches. Incidentally, I have deliberately omitted the White House, the United States Capitol and Mount Vernon, judging that they are too familiar to all Americans.

If you intend, as I do, to give every generation its chance, you will be struck by the impatience with which one decade looks at the achievements of another, and also by the disdain with which one area looks at another. We may be united as a nation, but we are disunited in the arts. New York City in the late nineteenth century was not eight hundred-odd miles from Chicago but eight million. At least that is the only conclusion to be drawn from a comparison of the work of Richard Morris Hunt and Stanford White with that of Louis Sullivan and Frank Lloyd Wright. Finally, the taste of no period is sacred for long. The colonial era may be enshrined in the minds of visitors to Williamsburg, but this was not always so. In 1848, when Louisa C. Tuthill published the first American history of architecture, she could not resist pointing out that colonial buildings were fortunately "all of such perishable materials that they will not much longer remain to annoy travelers *in search of the picturesque* through the beautiful villages of New England."

So we are setting out on a journey that will be rudely interrupted once we listen to critics with minds of their own. There are many of these. One was Thomas Jefferson, who might not have objected to curiosities like the remains of the Spanish Southwest, but would have wondered why anyone bothered with

Virginia in the early eighteenth century. "The genius of architecture seems to have shed its maledictions over this land," he remarked in 1784.

Jefferson expected, and he may have been right about this, that things would improve once he began to play architect himself. He did leave us Monticello, the Capitol of Virginia, and the incomparable campus of the University at Charlottesville. Strangely, not one of these buildings found favor with Ralph Adams Cram when he came to write his autobiography in 1936. For Cram, Jefferson was merely a dilettante who "severed design and style from construction and function." Had Cram taken a second look at the Federal Period, in which Jefferson played so prominent a part, he *might* have recognized that this dilettante was a revolutionary among other revolutionary architects, many of whom came from abroad to upset one parochial (or colonial) notion after another.

But Jefferson, who was unable to digest the novels of Sir Walter Scott, might have been perplexed by the Romantic Period from 1820 to 1860, when America was seduced by so many revivals, the Greek, the Gothic, the Egyptian and even the Moorish. Cram, so often out of sorts when not appraising his own work, was disgusted by the anarchy of what he termed Jacksonian Democracy. "Even the Dark Ages that followed the Fall of Rome could . . . show no parallel," he argued, "for even then such building as was done had at least the qualities of modesty and sincerity of purpose. The black years of American architecture revealed neither of these qualities; instead the product was vulgar, self-satisfied and pretentious, instinct with frontier ideology and as rampantly individualistic as the society it so admirably expressed."

For his part Emerson's earnest friend the sculptor Horatio Greenough boiled with indignation at the make-believe involved in a Grecian villa or a Gothic cottage, never once suspecting that the Gothic Revival would ultimately lead to what we call modern architecture in 1977. Andrew Jackson Downing, the Gothic prophet of those days, could on occasion talk strangely like Frank Lloyd Wright, as when he pleaded for expressing the nature of materials.

Once the Civil War was over, America was faced with the Venetian variety of Gothic that John Ruskin had been championing in England, and until quite recently solemn critics have been appalled by the uncompromising vitality of men like Furness & Hewitt, who gave us the Pennsylvania Academy of Fine Arts. We cannot overlook either the Venetian Gothic or the rage for the Mansardic Style that swept the country in those years. Long despised, the Mansardic Style has its admirers in our time who regret the disappearance of glorious hotels like the Grand Union in Saratoga.

Then came Henry Hobson Richardson, who brought order out of this fascinating chaos when he won the competition for Trinity Church, Boston, in 1872. Richardson was to conquer his generation, although Cram, who proves to be so often out of step, was horrified by his legacy. "There was neither grace nor sensibility, but there was power, and power was not enough," came Cram's verdict. He shuddered at his predecessor's predilection for the Romanesque.

Samuel Bing, the famous Parisian dealer in Art Nouveau, was more generous in his opinion of Richardson. Noting his suburban railroad stations on the visit he made to the United States in the 1890s, Bing reported that it was "astonishing to observe how the massive gravity of archaic forms, so dear to the entire Richardsonian school, has been adapted to this small structure, without sacrificing any visual pleasure or conformity to the desired rustic character. On occasion, a large bay, whose semi-circular arch springs directly from the ground, is opened in the compact and low masonry to provide a sheltered access for vehicles. No superfluous ornament, only the obvious effort to impart a sober and artistic flavor to the whole building, down to the most minute detail." Perhaps it was the glance Bing gave Richardson's gate lodge for Frederick L. Ames that led him to proclaim that "the American country house is low."

No one, however, understood Richardson more completely than his assistants Charles Follen McKim and Stanford White, who joined William Rutherford Mead in 1879 to form McKim, Mead & White, the most prestigious architectural firm in our history. In their early work in the so-called Shingle Style, based on the master's precedent, they even managed to surpass him in creating buildings that were ideally suited to their site as well as subtle, poetic statements of texture. In 1887, when McKim completed the summer house at Bristol, Rhode Island of William G. Low, the partners had gone far toward laying the foundations of modern architecture. Frank Lloyd Wright should have been the first to agree with this, for the shingled house he built for himself in Oak Park in 1889 owed much to what McKim had accomplished in Bristol.

But McKim, Mead & White's offices were in New York City, and the partners came to understand that here was a craving for splendor that could be satisfied by nothing less than a return to the inspiration of the Renaissance. Richard Morris Hunt, the first American to graduate from the Ecole des Beaux Arts, was the first to sense this need. In 1881 he gave his blessing to the outrageous social ambition of Mrs. W. K. Vanderbilt by designing for her the now vanished Early French Renaissance palace at 660 Fifth Avenue.

Hunt went on from palace to palace until his death in 1895, ending his career with the gigantic Biltmore at Asheville, North Carolina for George Washington Vanderbilt II. Whether his clients felt at home in their homes is a question. His interiors were more often overwhelming than comfortable.

In the end it was McKim, Mead & White and not Hunt who made over New York into a Renaissance city. This campaign began in 1885 when White laid out five adjoining town houses for the railroad promoter Henry Villard and four of his friends on Madison Avenue to the rear of Saint Patrick's Cathedral. This was no copy of the Cancelleria in Rome but a re-creation of the Italian Renaissance for the requirements of American millionaires. Its success was immediately recognized. McKim's chance came with the Boston Public Library of 1887. From this time on the partners worked their will wherever they wished in the East.

"Our clients got richer and richer," declared Stanford White's son, who paid no attention to the priggish modernists so anxious to bring up the question of guilt by association. The Swiss modernist Le Corbusier had a sense of humor: he was overjoyed by this rebirth of the Renaissance when he finally visited New York. "It's so well done," he exclaimed, "that it's almost as good as the real thing."

"Chicago is moving in the right direction and should be encouraged in every way," announced Mrs. Astor's great and good friend Ward McAllister when he inspected the World's Fair of 1893, intended by Hunt and McKim to acquaint the natives with the last word from New York. But Chicago had a few ideas of its own. It could also be as serious as New York was entertaining. "As a rule," said Marshall Field, the richest of all Chicagoans, "people do not know how to save." He did, and so did the packer P. D. Armour, who liked to get down to work "before the boys with the polished nails show up." This was the environment in which William Le Baron Jenney built the (since demolished) Home Insurance Building of 1883, generally considered to be the world's first skyscraper, i.e. the first tall building to exploit the steel frame.

This was also the environment in which Louis Sullivan turned skyscrapers into works of art. But although he and his partner Dankmar Adler produced the Auditorium of 1889, unquestionably the greatest opera house in the world, Sullivan was too much the idealist to cope with the spirit of Chicago.

Frank Lloyd Wright could.

Not content with being Sullivan's chief draftsman, Wright boasted of being "the best-paid draftsman in the city of Chicago." Here was the man to face the city head-on. "You've got to have guts to be an architect," he said. "People will come to you and tell you what they want, and you will have to give them what they need." More serious than Downing when it came to expressing the nature of materials, he believed that "democracy deserves something better than the box," and designed house after house in which space *actually* flowed for the self-made businessmen of the Middle West whom he idolized. (Actually is underlined for the very good reason that the *flow of space* is one of the favorite clichés of architectural historians. But Wright could tease a cliché into life.)

"I intend to be the greatest architect who ever lived," cried Wright, who was nothing if not an individualist. He was no admirer of Walter Gropius, who came to Harvard in 1937 after heading the Bauhaus in his native Germany. For Gropius architecture was teamwork. As the captain of the team he saw no reason for exposing his students to the perils of architectural history. "When the innocent beginner is introduced to the great achievements of the past," he explained, "he may be too easily discouraged from trying to create for himself."

Gropius's compatriot Ludwig Miës van der Rohe, landing in Chicago in 1938, preached somewhat the same gospel. "The individual is losing significance," he was fond of saying. "His destiny is no longer what interests us. The decisive achievements in all fields are impersonal, and their authors are for the most part obscure. They are part of the trend of our times toward anonymity." For all that, Miës was an artist, and the elegant, immaculate precision of his best work was a challenge to every architect who failed to take the proper pains.

But there was another type of architecture in California, less self-conscious than that of Gropius and Miës. There was the work of Harwell Hamilton Harris, who fought for what he called progressive regionalism. Aware of the marvelous inventions of Bernard Maybeck, who was not ashamed of his reverence for Roman temples, nor afraid of the wildest adventures with the Gothic, Harris was equally conscious of the explorations of the brothers Greene & Greene. They had learned much from the early work of McKim, Mead & White, had Greene & Greene, and their shingled bungalows from the years before the First World War proved that they were devoted to texture. Harris on his own was to display a joy in the sensuous quality of redwood that is one of his claims on the future.

Another great Californian was the undogmatic William Wilson Wurster. "There is always more than one answer to every question," he believed. Here was a philosophy that appealed to undogmatic clients in the Bay Area, and the hundreds of commissions won by the firm of Wurster, Bernardi & Emmons are the advertisement, if he needed one, that he knew his audience. These buildings slip so easily into the California scene that there is no sign of the effort required to seem so effortless.

"No one has ever asked me to design a *modern* house!" was the boast of one modern refugee from the East on the West Coast. The success of Charles W. Moore, of Benton Harbor, Michigan, who may be described as a refugee from the Middle West, testifies that architecture is still an open, not a closed world, in the California of 1977.

This is, of course, a biassed book. A book without bias is an encyclopedia. And an encyclopedia I had no intention of compiling.

And now may I remind everyone that a photograph is never a substitute for a building. Photographs are meant to be invitations to go and see for yourself, and if you accept my invitations, this may be counted a successful book.

Finally, I should like to thank Richard Schuler, Ernest Pile and their associates at Compo Photocolor, who have developed and enlarged my negatives for so many years and given me so much good advice. My gratitude also goes to Harry Ford of Atheneum, who designed not only this but the original edition, which was suggested by Simon Michael Bessie.

CONTENTS

San Estévan, Ácoma, New Mexico, 1642?(architect unknown). This Franciscan mission, atop a 357-foot mesa, was the site of Willa Cather's novel Death Comes for the Archbishop.

Nuestra Señora de la Asunción, Zia Pueblo, New Mexico, 1692 (architect unknown).
San Xavier del Bac, Tucson, Arizona, 1784–97 (architect unknown).
Like Nuestra Señora de la Asunción, San Xavier was built by Franciscans, but was unusually lavish.

San Francisco de Taos, Ranchos de Taos, New Mexico, c. 1772 (architect unknown). This too was a Franciscan mission.

ABOVE: *Saint Michael's Church, Charleston, South Carolina, 1761(architect unknown).* BELOW: *Drayton Hall near Charleston, South Carolina, c. 1738(architect unknown). Saint Michael's was one of the rare imposing churches of the colonial period. Drayton Hall was the seat of John Drayton, one of the members of His Majesty's Council.*

Residence of Miles Brewton, Charleston, South Carolina, c. 1769(architect unknown). The earnest New England patriot Josiah Quincy, Jr., who called on Brewton in 1773, was dismayed by the luxury of this town house, the finest in Charleston. Said Quincy of the Charleston aristocracy: "The gentlemen are mostly men of the turf and gamesters. Political inquiries and philosophical disquisitions are too laborious for them; they have no great passion for to shine and blaze in the forum or a senate."

In all likelihood we shall never know the names of the contrivers of most of our colonial buildings. Professional architects were unheard of until the late eighteenth century. The influence of the Italian Renaissance, carried to England by Inigo Jones and his successors, pervaded the colonies in the eighteenth century. The oustanding town and country houses—and possibly even an occasional church—were probably planned by enlightened men of leisure. With a book or two of plates of the latest architecture from Great Britain at his elbow, a dilettante (often the owner of an estate) could please himself and his descendants.

5

COLONIAL SOUTH CAROLINA

Exterior and interior of Saint James Church, Goose Creek, South Carolina, 1711 c.—interior c. 1790?(architect unknown). Here may be found the memorial to Ralph Izard, the only elegant expatriate of colonial times. A connoisseur of baroque and rococo music, he was disappointed in Italy when he found no music there to compare with that of Johann Christian Bach.

COLONIAL
VIRGINIA

*Westover, Residence of
William Byrd II, Charles
City County, Virginia,
c. 1730(architect
unknown).*

The grandson of a London goldsmith, William Byrd II sometimes forgot that he
was the descendant of a tradesman. "Luxury," he once wrote his factor in England, "is bad enough amongst people of quality, but when it gets among that
order of men that stand behind counters, they must turn cheats and pickpockets
to get it, and then the Lord have mercy on those who are obliged to trust to their
honesty." Carter Burwell was the grandson of Robert "King" Carter, the first
great real estate speculator in the New World.

*Carter's Grove,
Residence of Carter
Burwell, James City
County, Virginia,
c. 1751–53(architect
unknown).*

Stratford, Residence of Thomas Lee, Westmoreland County, Virginia, c. 1725 (architect unknown). In this—the most imposing of all colonial houses still intact—was born Thomas Lee's descendant Robert E. Lee.

OPPOSITE ABOVE: *The Governor's Palace, Williamsburg, Virginia, 1706–20 (architect unknown).* BELOW: *The Capitol, Williamsburg, Virginia, 1751–53 (architect unknown). Both were restored by the generosity of John D. Rockefeller, Jr., 1928–34.*

COLONIAL VIRGINIA

Christ Church, Lancaster County, Virginia, 1732(architect un-known). Here was buried Robert "King" Carter, founder of the Carter dynasty. Shirley was built for one of his descendants; so was Carter's Grove.

OPPOSITE ABOVE: *Shirley, Charles City County, Virginia, c. 1769 (architect unknown).* BELOW: *Mount Airy, Richmond County, Virginia, c. 1758(architect unknown). The mother of Robert E. Lee was born at Shirley. Mount Airy was the home of John Tayloe, who kept one of the few private race tracks in colonial America.*

COLONIAL VIRGINIA

COLONIAL
MARYLAND

ABOVE: *Hammond-Harwood house,
Annapolis, Maryland, 1770–74
(William Buckland)*. BELOW:
*Interior of dining-room, Hammond-
Harwood house. This was the
greatest achievement of architect
William Buckland.*

COLONIAL PENNSYLVANIA

ABOVE: *Mount Pleasant, Philadelphia, Pennsylvania, 1761–62 (architect unknown).*
BELOW: *Cliveden, Philadelphia, Pennsylvania, 1761 (architect unknown). These are the most eloquent examples extant of the wealth of Philadelphia when it was the most important city of the American colonies. The former was the home of the privateer James MacPherson, the latter of Chief Justice Benjamin Chew.*

Residence of Parson Joseph Capen, Topsfield, Massachusetts, c. 1683 (architect unknown). This is probably the finest remaining example of 17th century American domestic architecture. The model for such a frame house could easily have been found in the countryside of 17th century England.

ABOVE: *Doorway, Residence of Samuel Porter, Hadley, Massachusetts, c. 1757 (architect unknown).* BELOW: *Rocky Hill Meeting House, Amesbury, Massachusetts, 1785 (architect unknown). The broken pediment of the Porter house at Hadley is typical of the attempts at elegance in the Connecticut Valley prior to the Revolution. The Rocky Hill Meeting House—an oblong without a tower—is characteristic of the austere houses of worship of those who broke away from the Church of England.*

Interior and Exterior of Touro Synagogue, Newport, Rhode Island, 1759–63 (Peter Harrison).

OPPOSITE: *Christ Church, Cambridge, Massachusetts, 1761 (Peter Harrison).* ABOVE: *Interior. Harrison was the first American architect—that is, the first man to design buildings for others to erect.*

Redwood Library, Newport, Rhode Island, 1748 (Peter Harrison).

Residence of Zenas Cowles, Farmington, Connecticut, 1780 (William Sprats).

Cathedral of the Assumption, Baltimore, Maryland, 1806 (Benjamin Henry Latrobe).

OPPOSITE: *Capitol, Richmond, Virginia, 1785–92 (Thomas Jefferson). This, the first example in the modern world of a public building in the temple style, was modeled after the Maison Carrée in Nîmes. Reverence for the architecture of ancient Rome was widespread at the beginning of the 19th century.*

In this time our government was founded and consolidated and Washington, D.C. was laid out and built up. This was also the time in which American architecture came into its own.

The Federal Period was remarkable for the number of architects from abroad who settled in the United States and raised our standards. Thanks to their presence, the professional architect was no longer an oddity. From the West Indies came William Thornton, who provided the first design for the U.S. Capitol. From Ireland came James Hoban, who not only worked on the Capitol but designed the White House. From France came Pierre-Charles L'Enfant, who gave us the plan of Washington, Etienne-Sulpice Hallet, who collaborated on the Capitol, Maximilien Godefroy, who created the First Unitarian Church in Baltimore, Joseph-François Mangin, who joined the native American John McComb, Jr., on the New York City Hall, and Joseph-Jacques Ramée, who laid out Union College. From England came William Jay, who brightened Savannah, George Hadfield, who superintended the U.S. Capitol, and most important of all the architects of the Federal Period, Benjamin Henry Latrobe. Most of Latrobe's private houses have been destroyed, but his genius is not likely to be forgotten since he was the major architect in the building of the U.S. Capitol.

Of our native architects Thomas Jefferson was easily the most distinguished. There was also Charles Bulfinch, who is known to have attacked the traditional colonial floor plan of a central hall with two rooms on each side by building a house—now destroyed—which boasted an elliptical salon, a French innovation. Then there was Samuel McIntire, the carver-turned-architect of Salem, Massachusetts, whose square frame houses concealed rather elaborate interiors modeled after those of the brothers Adam in England. Finally Asher Benjamin, who published the first American builders' guides, could scarcely be overlooked.

ABOVE: *Monticello, Residence of Thomas Jefferson, Charlottesville, Virginia, 1770–1809 (Thomas Jefferson). Jefferson modeled his own house after the villas erected in 18th century England by the Earl of Burlington, who—like Jefferson— was especially fond of the work of the 16th century Italian Andrea Palladio. But Jefferson was shrewder than Burlington when it came to adapting Palladio to a non-Italian site.* BELOW: *Bremo, Residence of John Hartwell Cocke, Fluvanna County, Virginia, 1815–19(architect unknown). Cocke himself may have been the designer of this Jeffersonian country seat.*

THE FEDERAL PERIOD

ABOVE: *The Octagon, Residence of John Tayloe, Washington, D.C., 1800 (William Thornton). This town house by the designer of the first plan for the U.S. Capitol was later on the headquarters of the American Institute of Architects.*
BELOW: *Rotunda, University of Virginia, Charlottesville, Virginia, 1822–26 (Thomas Jefferson). The rotunda dominating this distinguished campus by Jefferson was later restored by Stanford White after a fire.*

ABOVE: *Residence of Nathaniel Russell, Charleston, South Carolina, c. 1811 (architect unknown).* BELOW: *Drawing Room.*

THE FEDERAL PERIOD

ABOVE: *Gardener's Cottage, and* BELOW: *Residence of Joseph Manigault, Charleston, South Carolina, 1790–97 (Gabriel Manigault). There were gentlemen of leisure who practiced architecture in the Federal Period; one of these was the Charlestonian Gabriel Manigault, son-in-law of Ralph Izard. In the gardener's cottage for his brother Joseph, Gabriel Manigault may have taken as his model one of the temples in the gardens of Stowe in 18th century England. The delicate interior of the house may have been inspired by the work of the brothers Adam.*

Dining Room, Residence of Joseph Manigault, Charleston, South Carolina, 1790–97 (Gabriel Manigault).

Residence of William Scarborough, Savannah, Georgia, c. 1818 (William Jay). One of the truly talented architects of the South in the Federal Period was the Englishman William Jay, who brought to Savannah something of the elegance of Regency England.

Hyde Hall, Residence of George Hyde Clark, Cooperstown, New York, 1811–13 (Philip Hooker). Philip Hooker of Schenectady, the designer of the old Capitol and City Hall at Albany (since replaced) fashioned this villa for an Englishman who was one of the great landowners of this section of New York State.

City Hall, New York City, 1811 (Joseph-François Mangin & John McComb, Jr.).
The elegant Louis XVI façade is obviously the contribution of Mangin.

Gore Place and Living Room, Residence of Christopher Gore, Waltham, Massachusetts, 1797–1804 (architect unknown). Although no one knows who designed this country seat for Governor Gore, the influence of Charles Bulfinch is unmistakable, for he was the one who introduced elliptical rooms in Federal New England.

Gardiner-White-Pingree house, Salem, Massachusetts, 1810 (Samuel McIntire). *A carver turned architect, McIntire was also responsible for the vanished house of Elias Hasket Derby, owner of* The Grand Turk, *the ship that proclaimed in 1787 that Salem was bidding for its share of trade with the Far East.*

ABOVE: *Church of Christ, Lancaster, Massachusetts, 1816 (Charles Bulfinch). One of the remarkable churches by the most remarkable architect of New England in the Federal Period. Architecture was originally a pastime for Bulfinch, who was born to wealth. He became a professional architect after going into bankruptcy.* BELOW: *State House, Boston, Massachusetts, 1795–98 (Charles Bulfinch). Sir William Chambers's Somerset House in London may have served as the model for the State House.*

Exterior and Interior of the Residence of Harrison Grey Otis, Boston, Massachusetts, 1796–97 (Charles Bulfinch). This was the first of three houses that Bulfinch planned for Otis, the Federalist politico.

Residence of Joseph Nightingale, Providence, Rhode Island, 1792(Caleb Ormsbee).

Residence of John Brown, Providence, Rhode Island, 1785(Joseph Brown). Providence in the Federal Period was one of the great architectural centers. A leading architect was Joseph Brown of the famous family of merchants; he designed this imposing mansion for his brother John.

35

Old West Church, Boston, Massachusetts, 1806 (Asher Benjamin). Converted into a branch of the public library, Old West is an excellent example of Benjamin's work. In 1797 Benjamin published The Country Builder's Assistant, *the first American handbook for carpenters and builders. Plate 33 of* The Country Builder's Assistant *was to inspire Lavius Fillmore (opposite page) when he designed the First Congregational Church at Bennington.*

First Congregational Church, Bennington, Vermont, 1806 (Lavius Fillmore).

THE FEDERAL PERIOD

THE ROMANTIC ERA 1820–1860

It was in the Romantic Era that the battle for modern architecture began. This may seem strange. The Romantic Era was the heyday of the Greek, the Gothic and many other revivals, and we all know that nothing seems more old-fashioned today than a return to the past, no matter what the excuse.

At first glance the romantics may seem innocent enough. Critics and architects alike, they were anxious to exploit the poetry of time past. But this was in the end a dangerous preoccupation. Though we may smile at the notion of a businessman traveling into the Middle Ages once he retired to his Gothic villa, this was the way the prestige of the Renaissance, which had held both England and 18th century America in its spell, was undermined. Once the prestige of the masters of the Renaissance was shattered, buildings could be planned, not to fit pre-conceived ideas of symmetry, but the desires of a growing family or business. The Gothic, by far the most vigorous of the romantic revivals, marked the end of the supremacy of the formal plan of the 18th century and the first step toward the planning-for-convenience of the 20th. Furthermore, once Gothic architecture was invested with mystery by the romantics, scholars could not help discovering the engineering achievements of the Middle Ages. And so the romantics reminded their descendants that architecture could be an adventure in engineering.

Both the Greek and the Gothic Revivals were of English origin. The former was launched in 1762 with the publication of Stuart and Revett's *Antiquities of Athens;* the latter was encouraged by the beginning of Horace Walpole's Gothic castle "Strawberry Hill" in 1750. It was Latrobe who introduced the Greek Revival—with the Bank of Pennsylvania (1799)—and the Gothic Revival—with William Crammond's house, Philadelphia (1799). These were too advanced for the taste of the Federal Period. But Latrobe's daring was an incentive to the romantics.

OPPOSITE ABOVE: *County Record (or Fireproof) Building, Charleston, South Carolina, 1822–27(Robert Mills).* BELOW: *Bethesda Presbyterian Church, Camden, South Carolina, 1820(Robert Mills). Mills, who studied under Latrobe after being encouraged by Jefferson, was the first American to be trained for the architectural profession. He later designed the Washington Monuments in Baltimore and Washington.*

ABOVE *and* OPPOSITE ABOVE: *Residence of H. K. Harral, Bridgeport, Connecticut, 1846 (Alexander Jackson Davis).* BELOW: *Interior of a bedroom. This Gothic villa, one of the greatest achievements of America's greatest romantic architect, was willed to the city of Bridgeport by the last owner, Archer C. Wheeler. In 1958 the Harral-Wheeler house was destroyed during the administration of Mayor Samuel Tedesco. The public protest was widespread, but futile.*

Capitol, Raleigh, North Carolina, 1831–33 (Town, Davis & Paton). Davis, who was nothing if not versatile, was as expert at the Greek Revival as at the Gothic. He collaborated on this, the most distinguished of all our state capitols, with Ithiel Town and David Paton.

Residence of Henry Delamater, Rhinebeck, New York, 1844(Alexander Jackson Davis). This Gothic cottage was designed for the local banker and built by local carpenters without the architect's supervision. His practice was so extensive that he could supervise only the most elaborate commissions.

Entrance Lodge to Llewellyn Park, West Orange, New Jersey, c. 1857(Alexander Jackson Davis). Davis made his own home in Llewellyn Park, a prize example of romantic planning laid out to suit the benevolent wholesale druggist Llewellyn Haskell.

Residence of W. J. Rotch, New Bedford, Massachusetts, 1850 (Alexander Jackson Davis).

Exterior and Dining Room of Lyndhurst, residence of William Paulding, Tarry-town, New York, 1838–65 (Alexander Jackson Davis). Lyndhurst was purchased in 1880 by the railroad financier Jay Gould, whose daughter was to present the mansion to the National Trust.

*Belmead, Residence of Philip St. George Cocke, Powhatan County, Virginia, 1845
(Alexander Jackson Davis). This Gothic villa (converted into a Roman Catholic
School for Negroes) was designed for General Cocke, who took his own life in
the Civil War, but not before he had helped Davis create the Gothic buildings for
the Virginia Military Institute at Lexington.*

THE ROMANTIC ERA

ABOVE: *New York Yacht Club, Hoboken, New Jersey, 1846(Alexander Jackson Davis)*. BELOW: *Residence of C. B. Sedgwick, Syracuse, New York, 1845(Alexander Jackson Davis). The Gothic clubhouse, which had been moved to Glen Cove, Long Island, when this picture was taken, has since been transplanted to Mystic, Connecticut. The Gothic house in Syracuse has been destroyed.*

Grace Church, New York City, 1846 (James Renwick, Jr.). One of the finest Gothic churches of the Romantic Era, this was designed by the only American architect to keep two steam yachts, one for cruising off the Florida coast, the other for voyages farther from home. He was only twenty-eight when this commission was completed. His mother was a Brevoort. His wife was an Aspinwall.

THE ROMANTIC ERA

Residence of C. T. Longstreet, Syracuse, New York, 1851 (James Renwick, Jr.). The Gothic castle at Syracuse (recently destroyed by Syracuse University) was designed for the first American to ship ready-made suits to the west coast.

Rectory, Grace Church, New York City, 1847 (James Renwick, Jr.).

Trinity Church, New York City, 1846 (Richard Upjohn). This Gothic structure, the greatest of all the churches of the Romantic Era, was designed by a high-minded native of England who had doubts about building churches for other than Episcopalians, and always insisted on what was proper for ritual use. He once designed a Presbyterian church. A rival observed that "he did it conscientiously, upon the ground that Presbyterians were not entitled to architecture."

Saint Mary's Church and Interior,
Burlington, New Jersey, 1846–54
(Richard Upjohn). This Gothic
church was designed for Bishop
George Washington Doane, whose
Italian villa by John Notman is
reproduced on page 55.

ABOVE: *Kingscote, Residence of George Noble Jones, Newport, Rhode Island, 1838 (Richard Upjohn).* BELOW: *Oaklands, Residence of R. H. Gardiner, Gardiner, Maine, 1835–36 (Richard Upjohn). The Gardiner castle was Upjohn's first significant commission. Kingscote was built for Gardiner's son-in-law. Note wing on the left of Kingscote. This was added by McKim, Mead & White in 1880. An interior view of the McKim, Mead & White wing is reproduced on page 93.*

ABOVE: *Whaler's Church, Sag Harbor, New York, 1844 (Minard Lafever)*. BELOW: *Residence of Benjamin Hunting, Sag Harbor, New York, 1845 (Minard Lafever). Lafever, a self-made architect who was once a carpenter was responsible for the rich Gothic of Holy Trinity on Brooklyn Heights, New York. He also published five handbooks for the guidance of builders. He was versatile, as may be seen from the contrast of the Grecian Hunting house and the Egyptian Whalers' Church whose steeple was lost in the hurricane of 1938.*

THE DEAD SHALL BE RAISED.

Grove Street Cemetery, New Haven, Connecticut, 1845–46 (Henry Austin). The Egyptian style was favored for the entrances of cemeteries, although one angry critic dismissed Egyptian architecture as fit for "embalmed cats and deified crocodiles."

Residence of Rt. Rev. George Washington Doane, Burlington, New Jersey, 1837 (John Notman). Presumably the first Italian villa erected in the United States, it has been destroyed.

ABOVE: *Second Bank of the United States, Philadelphia, Pennsylvania, 1818–24 (William Strickland).* BELOW: *Merchants' Exchange, Philadelphia, Pennsylvania, 1832–34 (William Strickland). Philadelphia was one of the great centers of the Greek Revival, and one of the leading Philadelphia architects was William Strickland who later designed the Grecian Capitol of Tennessee.*

Residence of Elias Brown, Old Mystic, Connecticut, 1835 (architect unknown).

Mitchell-Turner house, Milan, Ohio, c. 1828 (architect unknown).

57

Girard College, Philadelphia, Pennsylvania, 1833 (Thomas U. Walter).

OPPOSITE ABOVE: *Andalusia, Residence of Nicholas Biddle, Andalusia, Pennsylvania, 1833 (Thomas U. Walter & Nicholas Biddle).* ABOVE: *River Temple at Andalusia.* OPPOSITE BELOW: *Drawing Room, Andalusia.*

Usually remembered as the indomitable adversary of Andrew Jackson, Biddle was more than just the president of the Second Bank of the United States. "The two great truths of the world," he announced, "are the Bible and Grecian architecture." His own home, planned with the aid of Thomas Ustick Walter, who later completed the dome of the U.S. Capitol, was modeled after the Theseum at Athens. Biddle fought and won the good fight for the Grecian structure of Girard College. He announced, when victory was near, that "for the first time since Pericles architecture was introduced into city politics."

Oak Alley, Vacherie, Louisiana, c. 1836 (architect unknown). This was built for the planter J. T. Roman, brother of the Louisiana Governor André Roman.

Belle Grove, White Castle, Louisiana, 1857 (Henry Howard). This majestic ruin was leveled by fire after this negative was taken. The original owner was the planter John Andrews, Jr.

61

ABOVE: *Belle Meade, Residence of William Giles Harding, Nashville, Tennessee, 1853(William Strickland?).* BELOW: *Gaineswood, Residence of Nathan Bryan Whitfield, Demopolis, Alabama, 1842(architect unknown).*

Ruins of Windsor Plantation, Port Gibson, Mississippi, 1861 (architect unknown).

ABOVE: *Afton Villa, Residence of David Barrow, Saint Francisville, Louisiana, 1849(architect unknown).* BELOW: *Staunton Hill, Residence of Charles Bruce, Charlotte County, Virginia, 1848(John Johnson).*

Longwood, Residence of Haller Nutt, Natchez, Mississippi, 1860 (Samuel Sloan). This example of what might be termed a Moorish Revival was left uncompleted when the Civil War interrupted the owner's ambition. The architect was a Philadelphian who published a builders' guide.

Rattle & Snap, Residence of George Polk, Columbia, Tennessee,
1845 (architect unknown).

Greenwood, Residence of William Ruffin Barrow, Saint Francisville, Louisiana, c. 1830 (architect unknown).

Laing Stores, New York City, 1848 (James Bogardus). Bogardus patented the cast-iron frame construction used here. This building has been dismantled for erection elsewhere in New York City.

OPPOSITE ABOVE: *Berry Hill, Residence of James Coles Bruce, Halifax County, Virginia, 1845 (architect unknown).* BELOW: *Temple at Berry Hill.*

Tea House, Residence of General Mariano Vallejo, Sonoma, California, c. 1850 (architect unknown). The General's Gothic villa is said to have been built in New England and shipped to California.

Capitol, Nashville, Tennessee, 1854–59 (William Strickland).

"Wedding Cake" house, Kennebunk, Maine, c. 1800,
Gothic decoration added c. 1850(architect unknown).

OPPOSITE ABOVE: *Residence of John Schoolcraft, Jr., Guilderland,*
New York, c. 1804(architect unknown). BELOW: *"The Three*
Bricks," Nantucket, Massachusetts, 1837(architect unknown). Built
for the three sons of Joseph Starbuck—William, Matthew and
George.

Grand Union Hotel, Saratoga, New York, 1872(architect unknown). This ex-
ample of the mansardic style was destroyed shortly after this picture was taken.

During and after the Civil War our architects were not certain of which way to turn. The mansardic style, modeled after that of Paris in the Second Empire, was popular, and an attempt was made to propagate the Venetian Gothic advocated by John Ruskin in England. Many buildings in the Age of Indecision were brutal and confused, but only a snob could fail to recognize and admire the vitality of much of American architecture at this time.

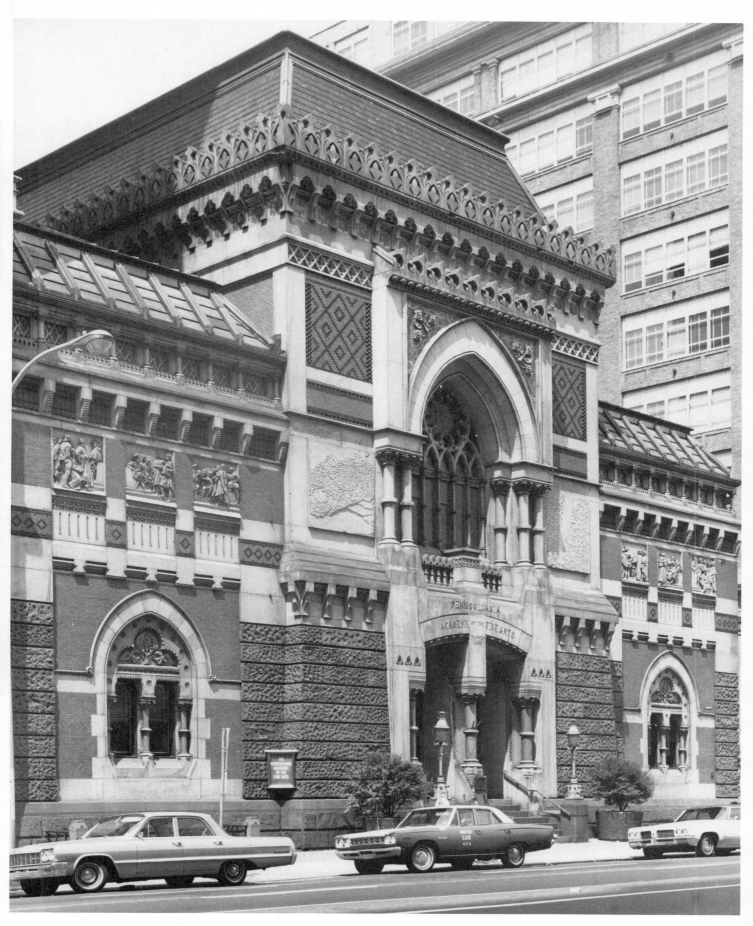

Pennsylvania Academy of Fine Arts, Philadelphia, Pennsylvania, 1872–76 (Furness & Hewitt). Furness, the indomitable Ruskinian of Philadelphia, hired Louis Sullivan before he showed up in Chicago.

Rooftop and Front Hall of Olana, Residence of the artist Frederic E. Church, Greendale-on-Hudson, New York, 1874 (Frederic E. Church & Calvert Vaux). This Moorish castle, set on a hill overlooking both the Catskills and the Berkshires, was the perfect retreat for a painter who specialized in remote volcanoes and icebergs.

THE AGE
OF
INDECISION

Hotel del Coronado, Coronado, California, 1886–88 (Reid & Reid).

Dining Room, Hotel del Coronado.

*Residence of E. J. "Lucky" Baldwin, Arcadia, California, c. 1875
(A. A. Bennett). Baldwin was a plunger in the Comstock Lode.*

OPPOSITE ABOVE: *Residence of William Carson, Eureka, California,
c. 1885 (S. & J. Newsom).* BELOW: *Vestibule, Residence of William
Carson, Eureka, California, c. 1885 (S. & J. Newsom).*

H. H. RICHARDSON

Henry Hobson Richardson, a native of Louisiana who graduated from Harvard College and studied at the École des Beaux Arts, was the genius who brought order to American architecture after the Civil War. The victim of a disease which cursed him with the waistline of a hippopotamus, he ate and drank with the bravery of a man who was well aware of his own death sentence, and he advertised his disdain for death by wearing bright yellow waistcoats.

The sculptor Augustus Saint-Gaudens, who knew and worshipped Richardson, has written that "although afflicted with a trouble for which he was absolutely prohibited stimulants, he once drank a quart of black coffee when on his way to Pittsburgh, in order to be in good condition when he met the committee to arrange for the building of that masterpiece, the jail and courthouse.

"At any rate, whenever I visited (him) . . . he would say before dinner: 'S-S-Saint-Gaudens, ordinarily I lead a life of abstinence, but tonight I am going to break my rule to celebrate your visit, you come so rarely.' He would thereupon order a magnum of champagne which, as none of the family drank it, had to be finished by him and me. . . . This had to be accompanied by cheese, which was also proscribed by the doctor, and of this he ate enormous quantities. The proceeding doubtless occurred every night, as he always managed to bring home a guest."

"There is a lot of work to do, isn't there?" Richardson once asked. "And *such* work! And to think that I may die here in this office at any moment." There were friends who marveled at the schooners of iced beer he downed in Venice, and declared that he would "never take the time to die." But he died on April 27, 1886, when not yet forty-eight. "The things I want most to design," he once protested, "are a grain elevator and the interior of a great river steamboat." He designed neither of these things, but he worked his will on American architecture as have few men before or since.

Trinity Church, Boston, Massachusetts, 1872–77. Superficially Romanesque in inspiration, Trinity Church was one of the great monuments of the 19th century. That a building could be so carefully composed was a lesson for the architects of the Age of Indecision. The porch was added in the 1890's by Richardson's successors, Shepley, Rutan & Coolidge.

City Hall, Albany, New York, 1880–81.

Residence of W. Watts Sherman, Newport, Rhode Island, 1874–76. The greatest of all Richardson's domestic designs was this house for William Watts Sherman, whose father had been a partner in the banking house of Duncan, Sherman & Co. In 1977 it houses an Old People's Home of the Baptist Church.

Ames Monument, Laramie, Wyoming, 1879. The Ames family of North Easton, Massachusetts were the greatest patrons of the architect. This is the monument he designed in memory of Oakes Ames and his brother Oliver Ames, Jr., who together financed the building of the Union Pacific Railroad. The sculptor Augustus Saint-Gaudens collaborated with the architect.

OPPOSITE ABOVE: *Oakes Ames Memorial Library, North Easton, Massachusetts, 1877–79.* BELOW: *Fireplace, Oakes Ames Memorial Library, North Easton, Massachusetts, 1877–79. Stanford White, then in the Richardson office, designed the fireplace, and Augustus Saint-Gaudens did the head of Oakes Ames.*

Crane Memorial Library, Quincy, Massachusetts, 1880–83.

Doorway, Residence of John J. Glessner, Chicago, Illinois, 1885–87 (H. H. Richardson).

Boston & Albany R. R. Station, Chestnut Hill, Massachusetts, 1884.

Gate Lodge, Residence of F. L. Ames, North Easton, Massachusetts, 1880–81.

Alleghany County Court House & Jail, Pittsburgh, Pennsylvania, 1884–87.

Residence of M. F. Stoughton, Cambridge, Massachusetts, 1882–83.
Mrs. Stoughton was the mother of the historian John Fiske.

OPPOSITE BELOW: *Interior, Residence of R. T. Paine, Waltham, Massachusetts,*
1886. Robert Treat Paine was the chairman of the building committee of Trinity
Church. He was also one of the original stockholders in the Calumet & Hecla
copper mines.

BURNHAM & ROOT

Reliance Building, Chicago, Illinois, 1890–95 (Burnham & Root) Burnham & Root were pre-eminent for years in designing Richardsonian skyscrapers in Chicago. One of their greatest skyscrapers, but with no trace of Richardson's influence, was the Reliance, which they entrusted to their draftsman C. B. Atwood.

MCKIM, MEAD & WHITE

One of the great events in the history of American architecture was the formation in 1879 of the firm of McKim, Mead & White. Charles Follen McKim, who had studied at Harvard and at the École des Beaux Arts, was trained in the office of H. H. Richardson, as was his partner Stanford White. William Rutherford Mead, the brother-in-law of William Dean Howells, was an Amherst graduate who traveled to Florence after getting his first training in the office of the Ruskinian Gothicist Russell Sturgis.

McKim, Mead & White began their career by designing a number of summer homes and casinos for summer resorts. Usually shingle-sheathed, these have weathered out the decades so gracefully that no one can doubt that their creators were supremely sensitive to the nature of materials. This is another way of saying that McKim, Mead & White in their early work must be numbered among the great modern architects.

ABOVE: *Stables, Residence of Cyrus Hall McCormick.* BELOW: *Residence of Cyrus Hall McCormick, Richfield Springs, New York, 1882.*

MCKIM, MEAD & WHITE

Dining Room, Kingscote, Newport, Rhode Island, 1880. This typical early McKim, Mead & White interior was an addition to the Gothic cottage designed by Richard Upjohn in 1838. The exterior of the cottage is reproduced on page 52.

OPPOSITE ABOVE: *Courtyard, Newport Casino, Newport, Rhode Island, 1881.* BELOW: *Exterior, Newport Casino. Like the Cyrus Hall McCormick house, the Newport Casino may be attributed to Stanford White, whose genius as a decorator could not be denied. Since this photograph was taken the Casino has been severely damaged by fire.*

Residence of Isaac Bell, Jr., Newport, Rhode Island, 1883. Bell was the brother-in-law of James Gordon Bennett, Jr., of The New York Herald, *for whom the firm of McKim, Mead & White created the Herald Building on Herald Square. Bennett was also the founder of the Newport Casino. Stanford White was the partner in charge of the Bell house.*

Residence of C. J. Osborn, Mamaroneck, New York, 1885. Stanford White was the partner responsible for this commission. The owner was the confidential broker of Jay Gould.

Casino, Short Hills, New Jersey, 1882.

Residence of Robert Goelet, Newport, Rhode Island, 1883. Very likely Stanford White was responsible for the Casino and the Goelet mansion, both of which bear the mark of his decorative genius.

96

MCKIM, MEAD & WHITE

Residence of W. G. Low, Bristol, Rhode Island, 1887. This, the most simple, and perhaps the most noble of all the early houses of the firm, must be attributed to McKim. It was destroyed because a later owner of the property fancied the house was not sufficiently "modern."

A revolution in American architecture occurred on the evening of March 26, 1883, when Mr. and Mrs. W. K. Vanderbilt gave their never-to-be-forgotten ball in their new and noble château by Richard Morris Hunt on the northwest corner of Fifth Avenue and 52nd Street, New York City. The château, now destroyed, proved that a millionaire could be superbly housed in a French Renaissance design.

This was a challenge that McKim, Mead & White could not ignore. Their answer was the finest house (or rather, houses) ever built in New York City: the complex of five adjoining mansions completed in 1885 for the railroad financier Henry Villard and four of his friends. Still standing on the east side of Madison Avenue between 50th and 51st Streets, the Villard mansions marked an abrupt reversal of the approach of McKim, Mead & White. The originality and spontaneity of the shingle style was discarded in favor of a return to the Renaissance for inspiration. But let no one think that the partners in their best work were dealers in second hand goods. In this instance the Cancelleria in Rome served as a model, but it would be silly to think of the Villard mansions as a copy. Rather, this was a palace re-created in the Renaissance style for the needs of an American millionaire and his associates. The draftsman Joseph M. Wells is said to have suggested this new trend, but Stanford White was the partner in charge. From this time forward McKim, Mead & White were famous for their reinterpretations of the Renaissance for American use.

Confronted with the two splendid achievements here shown, America surrendered to McKim, Mead & White, which became the most influential firm in the history of American architecture.

The Boston Public Library, Boston, Massachusetts, 1887. This was McKim's triumph, as the Villard houses were Stanford White's. It was inspired by the Italianate Bibliothèque Sainte-Geneviève in Paris, completed by Henri Labrouste in 1850, but again was no copy.

The northern wing of the Villard complex, New York City, 1885. The Villard houses are slated to be dismembered, the firm of Emery Roth & Sons having decided that a new hotel should be erected on this site.

The clock on the stairs of the southernmost house in the Villard complex, New York City, 1885. Originally occupied by Villard, later by Whitelaw Reid. Stanford White here collaborated with the sculptor Augustus Saint-Gaudens.

Interior, Pennsylvania Station, New York City 1903–1910. The Station was destroyed in 1963, but not before modernists like Philip Johnson and the widow of Eero Saarinen deplored its disappearance.

The Morgan Library, New York City, 1906.

Residence of E. D. Morgan, Newport, Rhode Island, 1891. E. D. Morgan, the grandson of New York's Civil War governor, was no relation of the banker J. P. Morgan of the library.

Four views of the Residence of Herman Oelrichs, Newport, Rhode Island, 1902. ABOVE: *Grand view;* BELOW: *Closeup;* OPPOSITE ABOVE: *Front hall;* BELOW: *Ball-room. Stanford White was responsible for this evocation of the Grand Trianon at Versailles.*

University Club, New York City, 1899. It was in McKim's University Club that J. P. Morgan met Charles M. Schwab at dinner on December 12, 1900. On March 3, 1901 Morgan announced that the founding of U.S. Steel could be no longer delayed.

MCKIM, MEAD & WHITE

Residence of James L. Breese, Southampton, Long Island, New York, 1906. This was one of Stanford White's last designs.

Richard Morris Hunt, the first American graduate of the École des Beaux Arts, was also the first American to solve the problem of the millionaire's home. The château he completed in New York City in 1881 for Mr. and Mrs. W. K. Vanderbilt—now destroyed—proved that the early French Renaissance was a congenial setting for the masters of America's new fortunes. The success of the W. K. Vanderbilt château sent McKim, Mead & White to the Renaissance for the inspiration of their later work.

The Breakers, which was one of Hunt's many expensive commissions, was planned for the grandson of Commodore Vanderbilt, founder of the New York Central System.

ABOVE: *The Breakers, Residence of Cornelius Vanderbilt II, Newport, Rhode Island, 1892–95;* BELOW: *Dining Room, The Breakers;* OPPOSITE: *Great Hall, The Breakers. This palace in the manner of 16th century Genoa is now open to the public.*

Marble House, Residence of Mr. and Mrs. W. K. Vanderbilt, New-
port, Rhode Island, 1893–95. Behind this Corinthian colonnade Mrs.
Vanderbilt plotted the marriage of her daughter Consuelo to the
ninth Duke of Marlborough.

ABOVE: *Dining Room, Marble House, Newport, Rhode Island, 1893–95. The portrait of Louis XIV has been attributed to Pierre Mignard.* BELOW: *Gold Room, Marble House, Newport, Rhode Island, 1893–95.*

109

ABOVE: *East view, Ochre Court, Residence of Ogden Goelet, Newport, Rhode Island, 1889–91.* BELOW: *West view. For this, perhaps the most successful of all his mansions, Hunt turned again to the early French Renaissance which had already inspired the W. K. Vanderbilt château in New York City. In 1977 Ochre Court is occupied by Salve Regina College.*

Biltmore, Residence of George Washington Vanderbilt II, Asheville, North Carolina, 1895. Biltmore, Henry James confessed, was "a thing of the high Rothschild manner." It was built for the brother of Cornelius Vanderbilt II and W. K. Vanderbilt.

CHARLES ADAMS PLATT

Residence of John Jay Chapman, Barrytown, New York, 1914 (Charles Adams Platt). Platt was an eminent rival of McKim, Mead & White. A sensitive student of the Renaissance, he designed this house for Stanford White's friend and admirer, the critic John Jay Chapman.

HORACE TRUMBAUER

Miramar, Residence of A. Hamilton Rice, Newport, Rhode Island, 1916 (Horace Trumbauer). Horace Trumbauer was famous as the architect for the Widener family of Philadelphia. Mrs. Rice had previously been married to George Dunton Widener, and the Widener Library at Harvard—in memory of her son who went down on the Titanic—was entrusted to the Trumbauer firm. Trumbauer is known to have stayed far away from the drafting room of his office. Miramar was probably designed by his draftsman Julian Abele, a gifted Negro who was obviously fond of the work of the great eighteenth century master Jacques-Ange Gabriel.

ABOVE: *Entrance*, BELOW: *Closeup, Hotel Ponce de León, Saint Augustine, Florida, 1885–88. Bernard R. Maybeck, later one of the great achitects of California, was in the Carrère & Hastings office at this time, and to him has been attributed the vivacity of this hotel. It was planned for H. M. Flagler, the first to appreciate Florida's possibilities as a winter resort. In 1977 the hotel is occupied by Flagler College.*

WARREN & WETMORE

Grand Central Station, New York City, 1903–13 (Warren & Wetmore, with the assistance of engineers Reed & Stem and Colonel William J. Wilgus.) Sculpture by Jules Coutan. This was intended to be the focal point, not only of Park Avenue, but of Manhattan Island. However, this brilliant essay in city planning received its death sentence in 1963, when Emery Roth & Sons, with the help of Walter Gropius and Pietro Belluschi, erected the mammoth Pan-Am Building between the station and the New York Central Building by Warren & Wetmore to the north.

JOHN & WASHINGTON ROEBLING

Brooklyn Bridge, Brooklyn, New York, 1867–83. The greatest engineering achievement of the 19th century, this was completed in the very year that Mr. and Mrs. W. K. Vanderbilt moved into their new château on Fifth Avenue.

Exterior and Detail, The Auditorium, Chicago, Illinois, 1889.

Stage Frame, The Auditorium, Chicago, Illinois, 1889.

ADLER & SULLIVAN

Too easily dismissed as the coiner of the unfortunate slogan "Form follows function," Louis Henry Sullivan was no mechanical functionalist, but an artist who understood that every successful building was the solution of a unique problem. With his partner Dankmar Adler, whose grasp of engineering and acoustics went unrivalled, Sullivan designed The Auditorium, a complex that included a hotel and the world's most distinguished opera house. The late Samuel Insull was responsible for the closing of the opera house and the removal of the Chicago Opera Company to a building he financed on the Chicago River. In 1977 the Auditorium houses Roosevelt University and the opera house, which has been meticulously restored by Harry M. Weese & Associates.

Decorative panel, The Guaranty Building. Sullivan was also a genius at the art of decoration, an art that has been overlooked by the contrivers of the skyscrapers in our own time.

ADLER & SULLIVAN

The Guaranty Building, Buffalo, New York, 1895.
As a designer of skyscrapers, Louis Sullivan has never been equalled.

*Carson, Pirie Scott & Company Building, Chicago, Illinois, 1899.
Now occupied by the department store of Carson, Pirie Scott &
Company, this building was planned for the firm of Schlesinger &
Mayer. Dankmar Adler had withdrawn from the partnership by
the time this commission was executed.*

Closeup, Carson, Pirie Scott & Company Building, Chicago, Illinois, 1899. Sullivan's faithful friend George Grant Elmslie is known to have sketched the ornamental work on this building.

Merchants' National Bank, Grinnell, Iowa, 1914. Depressed by the emphasis of the Chicago World's Fair of 1893 on the classical revival, Sullivan watched his practice dwindle in his last years. But there was no decline in the quality of his work.

Tomb of Carrie Eliza Getty, Graceland Cemetery, Chicago, Illinois, 1890.

LOUIS SULLIVAN

National Farmers' Bank, Owatonna, Minnesota, 1907–08. Sullivan's associate George Grant Elmslie is known to have assisted him on this masterpiece. Since this photograph was taken, the bank has been enlarged and restored by Harwell Hamilton Harris. In his restoration Harris has displayed a total understanding of Sullivan's aims.

ABOVE: *Residence of H. C. Bradley, Woods Hole, Massachusetts, 1912.* BELOW: *Interior of living room. In its adaptation to the site, and in its emphasis on the nature of materials, this seaside cottage recalls the great achievements of the early days of McKim, Mead & White. The firm of Purcell & Elmslie, which flourished in Chicago and Minneapolis in the early twentieth century, was formed by William Gray Purcell, a devoted admirer of Louis Sullivan, and George Grant Elmslie, Sullivan's friend to the end.*

125

Merchants National Bank, Winona, Minnesota, 1911.
George Feick was a partner in the firm when this bank was designed.

Residence of J. G. Melson, Mason City, Iowa, 1913. The designer of this house was one of the challenging architects of the Middle West in the early twentieth century. Trained in the office of Frank Lloyd Wright, Griffin won the international competition for the plan of Canberra, the capital of Australia, and spent his last years in Australia and India. Since this photograph was taken, the Melson house has been altered out of recognition.

WILLIAM DRUMMOND

River Forest Women's Club, River Forest, Illinois, 1913. William Drummond of the firm of Guenzel & Drummond was also trained in the office of Frank Lloyd Wright.

Exterior and Interior, Unity Temple, Oak Park, Illinois, 1906.

FRANK LLOYD WRIGHT

The most inventive and probably the greatest of all American architects was Sullivan's pupil Frank Lloyd Wright, who fought a lifelong battle for what he termed "organic architecture." A building, he held, should grow easily from its site and be designed from inside out. A champion of informal planning, he decided that walls should be screens instead of barriers. He also emphasized, with uncanny sympathy, the texture of whatever materials he used.

Wright was always aware of his own importance. He understood, as did no one else, that the wistful artist is no artist at all.

FRANK LLOYD WRIGHT

ABOVE: *Residence of Ward W. Willitts, Highland Park, Illinois, 1902.*

BELOW: *Residence of Frederick C. Robie, Chicago, Illinois, 190*

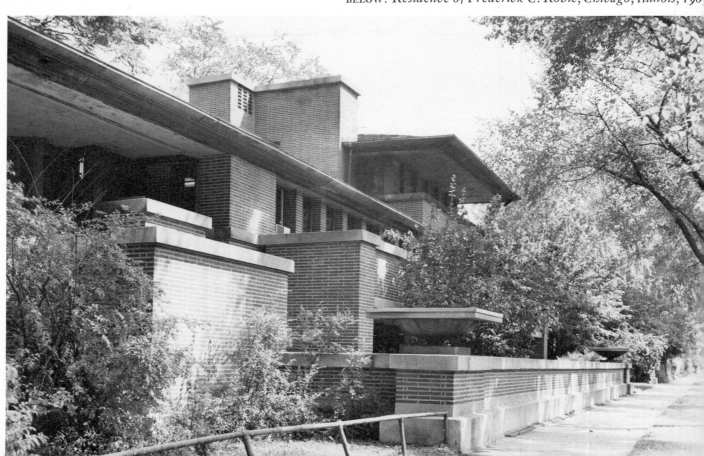

Residence of B. Harley Bradley, Kankakee, Illinois, 1900.

Playhouse for the children of Avery Coonley, Riverside, Illinois, 1912.

The Bradley house has been preserved as a restaurant, but the Coonley house has been altered out of recognition to be a home for five families. Even the playhouse for the Coonley children has been made over since this photograph was taken.

Residence of George Madison Millard, Pasadena, California, 1923.

Residence of Aline Barnsdall, Hollywood, California, 1920.

Exterior and Interior, Residence of H. T. Mossberg, South Bend, Indiana, 1952.

OPPOSITE ABOVE *and* ABOVE: *Falling Water, Residence of E. J. Kaufmann, Bear Run, Pennsylvania, 1936.* BELOW: *Interior, living room, Falling Water.*

FRANK LLOYD WRIGHT

OPPOSITE ABOVE: *Far view, Taliesin East, Residence of Frank Lloyd Wright, Spring Green, Wisconsin, 1925–59;* BELOW: *Entrance, Taliesin East;* ABOVE: *Interior, Studio, Taliesin East. Wright once observed that "no house should ever be* on *any hill or* on *anything. It should be* of *the hill, belonging to it, so hill and house should live together each the happier for the other."*

ABOVE: *Courtyard, Taliesin East, Residence of Frank Lloyd Wright, Spring Green, Wisconsin, 1925–59;* BELOW: *Mrs. Wright's wing, Taliesin East.*

FRANK LLOYD WRIGHT

ABOVE: *Office, Taliesin West, Residence of Frank Lloyd Wright,
Phoenix, Arizona, 1938–59.* BELOW: *Terrace, Taliesin West.*

ABOVE: *Drafting room, Taliesin West, Residence of Frank Lloyd Wright, Phoenix, Arizona, 1938–59.* BELOW: *Interior, Living room, Taliesin West.*

Research Tower, S. C. Johnson & Son, Racine, Wisconsin, 1951.

Interior and exterior, Administration Building, S. C. Johnson & Son, Racine, Wisconsin, 1939.

Exterior and interior, First Unitarian Meeting House, Madison, Wisconsin, 1951.   143

ABOVE: *Entrance Lodge and* BELOW: *Main House, Auldbrass Plantation, Residence of Leigh Stevens, Yemassee, South Carolina, 1940.*

144

FRANK LLOYD WRIGHT

*Closeup and full view, V. C. Morris Store,
San Francisco, California, 1949.*

FRANK LLOYD WRIGHT

The most remarkable campus to be laid out since Thomas Jefferson's University of Virginia is Florida Southern College.

Administration Building, Florida Southern College, Lakeland, Florida, 1948.

ABOVE: *Pfeiffer Chapel, Florida Southern College, Lakeland, Florida, 1940.*

BELOW: *Roux Library, Florida Southern College, Lakeland, Florida, 1942.*

Residence of Lowell Walter, Quasqueton, Iowa, 1949.

Boat house for Lowell Walter, Quasqueton, Iowa, 1949.

Residence of Douglas Grant, Cedar Rapids, Iowa, 1951.

Interior of the Central Hall, and two views of the exterior, Guggenheim Museum, New York City, 1959.

Residence of Mrs. Clinton Walker, Carmel, California, 1952.

Residence of David Wright, Phoenix, Arizona, 1952.

IRVING GILL

Residence of Miss Ellen Scripps, La Jolla, California, 1914.

If modern architects may be divided into two classes, those whose approach is impersonal and those whose approach is personal, Gill obviously belongs with the first group. In his disdain of all decoration he was close to the Viennese Adolf Loos. Like Frank Lloyd Wright, Gill was a graduate of Louis Sullivan's office.

Since this photograph was taken, the Scripps house has been remodeled by the local art museum which makes use of the building, and few traces remain of the architect's intentions. Gill was, however, one of the important architects of California in the early twentieth century, and before the remodeling was carried out this was one of his important buildings.

RICHARD J. NEUTRA

Residence of W. D. Tremaine, Santa Barbara, California, 1948.

Neutra is famous for the impersonal elegance of his designs. A graduate of the office of Adolf Loos in his native Vienna, Neutra settled in Los Angeles in 1925 after an apprenticeship with Erich Mendelsohn in Berlin and Holabird & Roche in Chicago.

OPPOSITE ABOVE: *Residence of Marcel Breuer, Lincoln, Massachusetts, 1939(Gropius & Breuer).* BELOW: *Residence of Gilbert Tompkins, Hewlett Harbor, Long Island, New York, 1946(Marcel Breuer).*

WALTER
GROPIUS

Walter Gropius, who directed the Brauhaus, a school of architecture and design in Weimar and Dessau in his native Germany, was made head of the Harvard School of Architecture in 1937. In America as in Germany he believed that "collective architectural work becomes possible only when every individual, prepared by proper schooling, is capable of understanding the idea of the whole, and thus has the means harmoniously to co-ordinate his independent, even if limited activity with the collective work." What this meant in plain English was made obvious when he joined Pietro Belluschi and Emery Roth & Sons in 1963 to design the Pan-Am Building in New York City.

MARCEL
BREUER

Marcel Breuer, Gropius's associate at the Bauhaus and at Harvard, followed in his footsteps in New York City, proposing a glass box on top of Grand Central.

Apartment Houses at 860 and 880 Lake Shore Drive, Chicago, Illinois, 1951.

LUDWIG MIËS VAN DER ROHE

Crown Hall, Illinois Institute of Technology, Chicago, Illinois, 1954.

Miës could be meticulous, as in this school of architecture building and in the apartment towers on the opposite page. The firm of Skidmore, Owings & Merrill, responsible for Grover Hermann Hall and the Crerar Library on the I.I.T. Campus, could not rise to his level.

A graduate of the office of Peter Behrens in Berlin, Miës headed the Bauhaus at Dessau after the resignation of Walter Gropius. He tried to be true to the ideal he set for himself in 1924. "The whole trend of our time," he then wrote, "is toward the secular. The endeavors of the mystics will be remembered as mere episodes. Despite our greater understanding of life, we shall build no cathedrals. Nor do the brave gestures of the romantics mean anything to us, for behind them we detect the empty form. . . . The individual is losing significance; his destiny is no longer what interests us. The decisive achievements in all fields are impersonal, and their authors are for the most part obscure. They are part of the trend of our times toward anonymity."

157

Residence of Philip Johnson, New Canaan, Connecticut, 1948.

A brilliant propagandist for the architecture of Walter Gropius and Ludwig Miës van der Rohe, Johnson went into the profession after establishing himself as a critic. He was associated with Miës in the design of the Seagram Building, New York City, 1955.

ALBERT KAHN

ABOVE: *General Motors Building, Detroit, Michigan, 1920.*
BELOW: *Coke ovens and blast furnaces, River Rouge Ford Plant, Dearborn, Michigan, c. 1921.*

Indisputably modern in his factories for Ford, Chrysler and General Motors, Kahn held fast to the belief that evolution was preferable to revolution in architecture. He followed the classical precedent of the Chicagoan Daniel H. Burnham when he designed Detroit's greatest monument, the General Motors Building.

Exterior and Interior, Library, Exeter Academy, Exeter, New Hampshire, 1972.

LOUIS I. KAHN

Salk Center, La Jolla, California, 1959–62.

No relation of Albert Kahn, Louis I. Kahn, a native of Esthonia, brought a Baltic austerity to American architecture in the 1960s and 70s.

Interior, Styling Building, General Motors Technical Center, Warren, Michigan, 1952 (Eero Saarinen & Associates).

"Our architecture," observed Eero Saarinen, "is too humble. It should be prouder, much richer and larger than we see it today." Before his death in 1961, when only fifty, he did much to realize that ambition. Beginning as the disciple of his father Eliel Saarinen, the Finn who created the subtle Kingswood School at Cranbrook, Bloomfield Hills, Michigan, he was to pay his respects to Miës in the General Motors Technical Center but emphasized, as Miës would not, the element of color in the glazed brick façades. Later on, in the Dulles Airport and the TWA Terminal at Kennedy, he would revel, as would Le Corbusier in France, in architecture as sculpture.

Closeup and far view, Styling Building, General Motors Technical Center, Warren, Michigan, 1952 (Eero Saarinen & Associates). The sculpture is the work of Antoine Pevsner.

ABOVE: *John Deere Administration Building, Moline, Illinois, 1964.*
BELOW: *John Foster Dulles Airport, Chantilly, Virginia, 1963.*

Exterior and Interior, TWA Terminal, Kennedy Airport, New York City, 1962.

Two views of the East Senior High School, Columbus, Indiana, 1972.

This school, which must be considered the prize exhibit of all the modern buildings of Columbus, Indiana, is the achievement of Ehrman Burkman Mitchell, Jr., trained at the University of Pennsylvania, and of Romaldo Giurgola, a native of Rome who has become Ware Professor at Columbia University.

BERNARD R. MAYBECK

Palace of Fine Arts, San Francisco, California, 1915. This master-piece from the Panama-Pacific Exposition was created by a graduate of the École des Beaux Arts who worked in the office of Carrère & Hastings before moving to California. "The keynote of a Fine Arts Palace," Maybeck claimed, "should be that of sadness, modified by the feeling that beauty has a soothing influence. . . . Great examples of melancholy in architecture and gardens may be seen in the engravings of Piranesi . . . whose remarkable work conveys the sad minor notes of old Roman ruins covered with bushes and trees."

First Church of Christ Scientist, and interior, Berkeley, California, 1912. This church suggests that there may be more to modern architecture than glass walls and steel frames.

Residence of Charles M. Pratt, Ojai, California, c. 1910.

The brothers Charles Sumner and Henry Mather Greene were natives of Saint Louis. After graduating from the Manual Training School of Washington University and the Massachusetts Institute of Technology, they settled in Southern California and made it plain that no one was more expert than they in emphasizing the texture of timber.

Residence of David B. Gamble, Pasadena, California, 1909.

Residence of C. H. Wolfe, Catalina Island, California, 1928.

A student of Otto Wagner in his native Vienna, Schindler went to work for
Frank Lloyd Wright before setting up his own office in Los Angeles. To the
end of his life (he died in 1953) he fought against the impersonal gospel of
Walter Gropius and Miës van der Rohe.

HARWELL HAMILTON HARRIS

Residence of Clarence Wyle, Ojai, California, 1948.

Harris is the Californian who has given new meaning to the great tradition of Maybeck and the brothers Greene & Greene.

Exterior and living room, Residence of Weston Havens, Berkeley, California, 1941. One of the great houses of the twentieth century, it commands but does not dictate to, an amazing view of San Francisco and the Bay and Golden Gate Bridges.

HARWELL HAMILTON HARRIS

Residence of Ralph Johnson, Los Angeles, California, 1949.

WILLIAM WILSON WURSTER

Two views, Residence of Warren Gregory, Santa Cruz, California, 1927.

Offices of Schuckl & Company, Canners, Sunnyvale, California, 1942.

WILLIAM WILSON WURSTER

In Wurster's eyes, the designer of a house enjoyed a rare privilege. "Families heading for the divorce courts don't build houses," he has said. "Houses are built by husbands and wives in the happiest period of their lives, and architects, unlike lawyers or doctors, have to be thankful that they are dealing with optimists."

Residence of I. Schuman, Woodside, California, 1949.

"There is," said William Wilson Wurster, "always more than one answer." He was never dogmatic. This may have been one reason for the enormous practice of the firm of Wurster, Bernardi & Emmons which he founded in 1945. Once head of the School of Architecture at the Massachusetts Institute of Technology, and later of the School of Architecture at the University of California at Berkeley, he died in 1973.

Center for Advanced Study in the Behavioral Sciences, Palo Alto, California, 1954. The Center is only of many examples of Wurster's skill in blending a building with its site.

Exterior and Interior, Residence of P. M. Klotz, Westerly, Rhode Island, 1969.

Condominium #1, Sea Ranch, California, 1965.

The complete credit line should read: Moore, Lyndon, Turnbull & Whitaker. When asked why he wanted to get away from the slickness of the International Style—symbolized by the doctrine of Walter Gropius at Harvard—Moore answered: "Because I don't think it is a very useful, interesting, meaningful description of what's going on. It's like the prepared statement of a politician."

CONCISE BIBLIOGRAPHY

Baldwin, Charles C., *Stanford White*, New York, 1931

Beirne, Rosamund R., et al., *William Buckland*, Baltimore, 1958

Benjamin, Asher, *The Country Builder's Assistant*, Boston, 1798

Bogardus, James, *Cast Iron Buildings*, New York, 1956

Bridenbaugh, Carl, *Peter Harrison*, Chapel Hill, 1949

Brooks, H. Allen, *The Prairie School*, Toronto, 1972

Burnham, Alan, "The New York Architecture of Richard Morris Hunt," *Journal of the Society of Architectural Historians*, May, 1952

————, ed., *New York City Landmarks*, Middletown, 1963

Columbus Area Chamber of Commerce, *Architecture of Columbus*, Columbus, 1974

Condit, Carl W., *American Building Art: Nineteenth Century*, New York, 1960

————, *American Building Art: Twentieth Century*, New York, 1961

Cook, John W. et al., eds., *Conversations with Architects*, New York, 1973

Cortissoz, Royal, *Monograph of the Work of Charles A. Platt*, New York, 1913

DaCosta, Beverley, *Historic Houses of America Open to the Public*, New York, 1971

Downing, Andrew J., *The Architecture of Country Houses*, New York, 1858

Downing, Antoinette F. and Scully, Vincent, Jr., *The Architectural Heritage of Newport, Rhode Island*, Cambridge, 1952

Eaton, Leonard K., *Two Chicago Architects and Their Clients*, Cambridge, 1969

Farr, Finis, *Frank Lloyd Wright*, New York, 1961

Ferry, W. Hawkins, *The .Buildings of Detroit*, Detroit, 1968

————, ed., *The Legacy of Albert Kahn*, Detroit, 1970

Gallagher, H. M. Pierce, *Robert Mills*, New York, 1935

Gebhard, David, *Architecture of Purcell & Elmslie*, Palos Park, 1974

————, *Schindler*, New York, 1972

————, et al., *A Guide to Architecture in San Francisco and Northern California*, Santa Barbara, 1973

————, *A Guide to Architecture in Southern California*, Los Angeles, 1964

Gideon, Sigfried, *Walter Gropius: Work and Teamwork*, New York, 1954

Gilchrist, Agnes A., *William Strickland*, Philadelphia, 1950

Gray, David, *Thomas Hastings Architect*, Boston, 1933

Guinness, Desmond, et al., *Thomas Jefferson Architect*, New York, 1973

Hamlin, Talbot F., *Benjamin Henry Latrobe*, New York, 1955

————, *Greek Revival Architecture in America*, New York, 1944

Harris, Harwell Hamilton, *Collection of His Writings and Buildings*, Raleigh, 1965

Hines, Thomas S., *Burnham of Chicago*, New York, 1974

Hitchcock, Henry Russell, *The Architecture of H. H. Richardson and His Times*, New York, 1936

————, *In the Nature of Materials: The Buildings of Frank Lloyd Wright*, New York, 1942

————, ed., *Philip Johnson Architect*, New York, 1966

Hoffmann, Donald, *The Architecture of John W. Root*, Baltimore, 1972

————, ed., *The Meanings of Architecture: Buildings and Writings by John W. Root*, New York, 1967

Johnson, Philip, *Ludwig Miës van der Rohe*, New York, 1953

Jordy, William H., *American Buildings and Their Architects*, Vols. 3 & 4, New York, 1972

————, et al., eds., *Montgomery Schuyler: American Architecture and Other Writings*, 2 Volumes, Cambridge, 1961

Kimball, Fiske, *Thomas Jefferson Architect*, Boston, 1916

————, *Mr. Samuel McIntire, Carver*, Portland, 1940

Kirker, Harold, *The Architecture of Charles Bulfinch*, Cambridge, 1969

————, *California's Architectural Frontier*, Santa Barbara, 1973

———— and James, *Bulfinch's Boston*, New York, 1964

Koch, Robert, ed., *Artistic America: Tiffany Glass and Art Nouveau Samuel Bing*, Cambridge, 1970

Landy, Jacob, *Minard Lafever*, New York, 1970

Laughlin, Clarence J., *Ghosts Along The Mississippi*, New York, 1948

McCoy, Esther, *Five California Architects*, New York, 1975

————, *Richard Neutra*, New York, 1967

Monroe, Harriet, *John Wellborn Root*, Boston, 1896

Moore, Charles, *Daniel H. Burnham*, 2 v., Boston, 1921

————, *Charles Follen McKim*, Boston, 1929

Moore, Charles W., et al., *The Place of Houses*, New York, 1974

Morrison, Hugh S., *Early American Architecture*, New York, 1952

————, *Louis Sullivan*, New York, 1935

Newcomb, Rexford G., *Architecture in Old Kentucky*, Urbana, 1953

————, *Spanish Colonial Architecture in the United States*, New York, 1937

O'Gorman, James F., ed., *Architecture of Frank Furness*, Philadelphia, 1973

Saarinen, Aline, ed., *Eero Saarinen On His Work*, New Haven, 1968

Scully, Vincent J., *Louis I. Kahn*, New York, 1962

————, *Shingle Style and the Stick Style*, New Haven, 1971

Steinman, David B., *The Builders of the Bridge*, New York, 1945

Sullivan, Louis H., *The Autobiography of an Idea*, New York, 1949

Temko, Allan, *Eero Saarinen*, New York, 1966

Upjohn, Everard M., *Richard Upjohn, Architect and Churchman*, New York, 1939

Warren, William L., "William Sprats and His Civil and Ecclesiastical Architecture in New England," *Old Time New England*, January-April, 1954

Wright, Frank Lloyd, *An Autobiography*, New York, 1932

INDEX (ARCHITECTS IN ITALICS)

WAYNE ANDREWS

Wayne Andrews was born in Kenilworth, Illinois, in 1913. He has been Archives of American Art Professor at Wayne State University since 1964. A graduate of Harvard, he earned his doctorate under Allan Nevins at Columbia. He was formerly Curator of Manuscripts at the New-York Historical Society and an editor at Charles Scribner's Sons; he was chosen Phi Beta Kappa Visiting Lecturer in 1975-6. He is the author of many books, including three companion volumes to the present one: *Architecture in Chicago and Mid-America*, *Architecture in New York* and *Architecture in New England*; *American Gothic* is an examination of the Gothic Revival in modern architecture; other books in American history include *The Vanderbilt Legend* and *Battle for Chicago*; he has also written *Germaine*, a biography of Madame de Staël, and a study of German literature and history, *Siegfried's Curse: The German Journey from Nietzsche to Hesse*. Mr. Andrews has contributed to such publications as *The Architectural Review*, *Town and Country*, *Harper's Bazaar* and *The New York Times*.